Whispers Across Tongues

Jill Somani

India | USA | UK

Made with ❤ on the BookLeaf Publishing Platform
www.bookleafpub.in
www.bookleafpub.com

To those who see the world through words,

To the voice that echoes through memories and dreams,

To the bonds that withstand time, trials and change,

For those who carry promises unspoken, and the stories that transcend borders.

Acknowledgements

I want to express my sincere gratitude to BookLeaf Publishing and their fantastic team for creating the #TheWriteAngle Writing Challenge. Such opportunities encouraged us through the journey from being a writer to becoming an author. Writing all the poetry and seeing the book reach readers and poetry enthusiasts has been a wholesome journey.

To my mother, words can never express how much she has shaped me—through the countless examples she sets for me to become a strong person, and the unwavering support she provides. I will always believe in the universe and the spirits of my maternal and paternal grandmothers.

To Raj, we started with a mutual passion for writing and ended with you letting me eat your brain while editing this book.

I am also grateful to the fellow writers I have met online since 2020 as a result of the COVID-19 pandemic and to the people I have met in Dublin for their ongoing inspiration to write the book. Such intense passion must reach the other side of the world and act as a reminder that no form of creativity is less competent.

Preface

Dear Readers and Enthusiasts,

This book is a collection of poems exploring the emotions of self-doubt, friendships, love and hope, dreams and vision, heartbreak, and, most importantly confidence. In each line, I have endeavored to capture the peaks and valleys of the universal moments that connect us all. These poems are fragments of a shared human experience—of wandering, finding, and becoming. I invite you to pause, think, and reflect on your paths, and perhaps find your own story echoed within these verses.

Whispers Across Tongues is about the voices we all carry within us—the ones we silence, the ones we nurture, the ones that grow louder with time and courage. This is an invitation to open yourself to those whispers, to let them guide you toward the person you are yet to become. May each poem be a small light, a breath of understanding, a quiet nod that you are not alone on your journey.

INDEX

PART TWO - THE ECHOES

Gratitude to my Readers

Ground,
Full of particles,
Mind,
Full of thoughts,
I wish,
A beautiful mosaic can be seen.

Part One – The Whispers

1. That Moon Light

It was a dark night,
As the dawn arrived,
Rough as a tree's bark,
All leaves shed.

Tick-tock,
Tick-tock,
Everything passed,
Locking the past.

Hugging some,
Piling up the dome,
As the moonlit,
Siren announced.

You are steady,
Always ready,
With those warm talks,
As sorted like a class.

2. The Shades of Horizon

Like a natural line,
I see you,
You are so far as I come near,
Always with the best clarity.

You are not that person,
Yet you stay always invariable,
Sharing the strongest bond,
Probably I've ever had with anyone.

Providing the brightest light,
Outgoing all boundaries,
I want you more,
Along with the waves of water,
Glittering under the sun.

3. Petals of Your Presence

I see you each day,
Wanting to lay,
Beside you, each day,
Like soft hay.

I see you each day,
Lost in the wonders of you,
Into those beautiful eyes,
Wondering how deep you are.

Your constant smile,
Resembling a peaceful isle,
Your all-time embracing arms,
Want me to hug you and sleep.

Mesmerized in your cuteness,
Regardless of your size,
Eviting the spoken species around me,
And that's how I see you.

4. That Kind of Ship

I saw two strangers,
Walking towards each other,
With hands full of good wishes,
Like each other's lashes,
Surely, they exchanged a few words,
As their faces glowed with calmness.

Two overwhelming souls,
Drenched in the warmth of light,
Commonly met their dogs too,
Exploring their ship, where,
Lived their chemistry,
Beyond the history.

5. A Probable Symphony

I don't think of you,
Consciously,
I don't think of you,
Intentionally,
Simply,
You are always weird to me,
"Hello" is uttered,
And I wonder,
If you really want to talk to me,
Or is it a possible blunder,
For the future to be.

6. The Colour Palette of Nature

Blue skies,
Pink blossoms,
White ice,
Black sky.

Mesmerizing,
Is the combination,
What if,
All is cast through the prism's charm.

Will the beauty,
Be lost,
Forever or temporary?

7. Weathering the Whirlpool

Leaking through,
The cracks no one notices,
A drum that is too swollen,
To hold its own,
Emotions ordered the shutdown,
Standing alone in silence,
The air scorches,
Pulling thoughts from the head.

Until the energy collapses,
Into a quiet void,
We wait,
Into the adrift of uncertainty,
Once again, the silence spoke,
Learning to stand,
A flicker of resolve,
Small yet unyielding.

To build doors, taller than our doubts,
And though the swirl remains,
We anchor ourselves,
Steady, ready to rise.

8. Sweets, Spices, and Senses

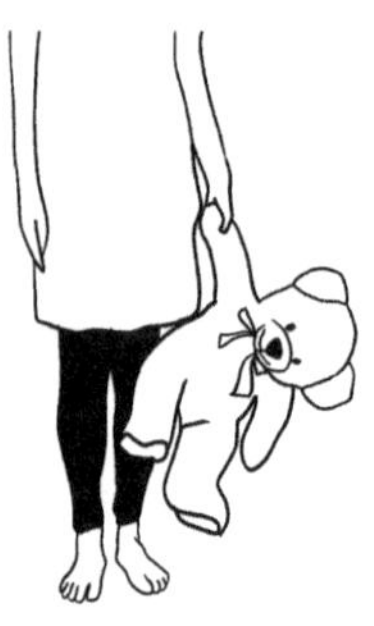

Where the memories live,
The soul sparks,
And that light ignites,
Which,
Never fails to realize,
How lively we are,
Hidden messages,
Or maybe revelations,
Wrapped with spicy sauces,
Or loathed with sour moments,
All kinds of flavours,
They fulfilled,
And,
A nostalgic candy it was.

9. Universe's Charm

Under the cool breeze,
I wait for you,
Like a paper without crease,
Waiting to write.

When the moonlight,
Touched the ground,
It made everything bright,
Similar to white roses.

The crickets humming,
The dogs barking,
The wolf crying,
Meanwhile,
I knew the universe was conspiring.

10. The Squared Emotion

Hey you,
You have been silent,
All this way,
I am sorry.

Rushed like a high tide,
Pulled like a low tide,
I lost my shore,
Between the illusion.

Standing all alone,
I faced unanswered,
Unknown allegations,
Nonetheless.

Seems I learned,
My lesson,
At all times,
Yet waiting for a forever still.

11. Beyond the Cracked Mirrors

Years passed by,
The pain was still the same,
Neither did it become easy,
Nor did it blur,
It had the strongest impact,
Piling up the sleepless nights,
That feeling never left,
Those faces could still be seen,
Touch could still be felt,
Warding off all weaknesses,
They stood like a shield,
No matter the distance apart,
They were still with me,
Along with my innocence.

12. The Language of Growing Secrets

Fingers tingling,
Throat drying,
Butterflies all over,
Whirled into the dark,
Some habits proved the mettle,
Passing through,
She made the way,
Measuring the perfect path,
Harder was the support,
Toughest was the faith,
Not letting their efforts go to waste.

13. Where the Heart Hesitates

The sinking heart,
All that time,
I waited for the unforeseen,
You never understood me,
Did I always demand more?

The sinking heart,
With everyone and everything,
I shouted myself out—
Out of the competition,
Having maniacal ideas.

The sinking heart,
Losing everything that I never gained,
Losing all that I overcome,
Losing the never-had social contact,
No! I never demanded more.

14. Heartache or Heartbreak?

It was the darkest shade of black,
Watery and moist,
Seconds, minutes, and hours,
All flew by,
It was nothing towards inertia,
Yet, they never moved,
Was that a heartache or a heartbreak?
Even the experts said nothing,
But,
Nothing was unexpected,
It was an eerie shadow,
Squeaking close the unwanted
windows.

15. Stepping into the Storm

So many already scribbled,
So much crooked,
There is no turning back,
As rare as common sense,
I am done,
Listening, Loathing,
Confessing, Crying,
And,
I found the answer,
Of?
''To be or not to be'',
Swirled into the storm of being,
I saw the last supernatural sapiens,
Who,
Soon lost life,
Within the sole soul.

16. Tethering Gold

Like unwanted insects on the farm,
I searched for those memories in the
barn,
Not seeing a glimpse,
It was as direct as a string.
I felt,
That a big part of me vanished,
Which couldn't even be forcefully glued.

Everything was so blurred,
More damage couldn't be incurred,
Waiting for that moment,
Lost were several memories.

Like the leaves in autumn,
My memories also fell apart,
I think about the marvel of the new
country,
Which made me feel so gloomy.

I promised to stay in touch,
With my fellow sweet souls,
We are close-knit yet distant,
Despite those kind moments,
Will they ever come back to me,
Or like everything else,
They will turn into ashes?

17. Is Reality the Illusion?

I see some illusions,
From the shore,
Whooshing around,
Vacuum stays the same,
A lot to feel,
A lot to communicate,
A lot to understand,
A lot to ponder,
Together,
Waiting, as the lame,
Absent in the present environment,
Trying not to be a bore,
I see the real.

18. Five Thousand Miles

Miles apart,
Same heart, pure soul,
Same connections, pure intentions.

Miles apart,
Intensity changes,
Deeper grows the fondness of wanting.

With one thing always,
Wishing for more,
Nobody cared about the final output.

19. The New Autumn

Both of them,
Imagining their tiny world,
Unknown to the harsh realities,
They brush past the barriers aside.

Like the flowers falling in winter,
She was a silent soul,
Whereas,
He wanted to be the new phase.

Her purest form became dark,
His dark became the deepest secret,
They failed to defend the innocence,
Losing their carefree expressions.

Although, they made some connections,
Both were scared of the accusations,
He evited his reactions,
With the dilemma.

Neither was her first exam nor was it
his,
It was some realization,
Tying them forever,

Regardless of the hurdles.

20. To, You I Have Yet to Meet

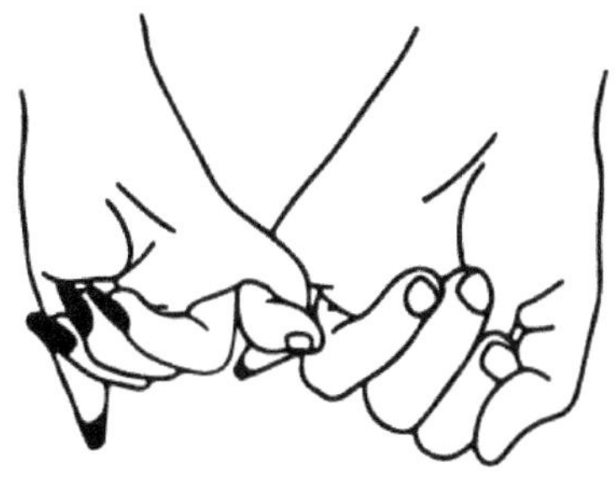

No one reads the core,
Nor will they know your soul,
No one will support you as you expect,
Or want you to be perfectly correct.

Not marking the stop,
Make sure you march till the end,
Not listening to what anyone drops,
Keep going where you wish to land.

Ruling over a small world,
I want to stand with you,
Till the eternity of our existence,
No matter where our abode is.

Meeting several people,
Through comfort and discomfort,
I will be our cushion to the sharp
wounds,
With only a little sweetness to impart.

21. A Voice from the Noise

Giggles and riddles,
Huddles and cuddles,
It is a limitless bubble,
Along with the innocence,
Clock changed,
Longing for the warmth,
From you,
With you,
For you,
Creating our bundle,
No less than the miniature,
With the gigantic persona,
It will always remind me,
Of your charisma,
All again.

You know what you don't know,
You don't know beyond what you know,
You keep knowing to know the space
within.

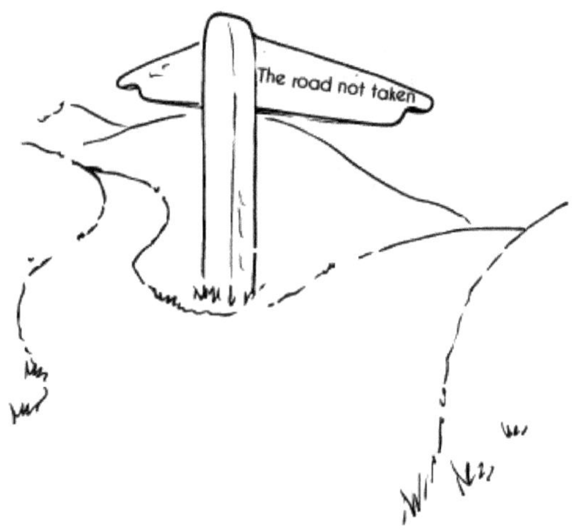

Part Two – The Echoes

1. There She Was

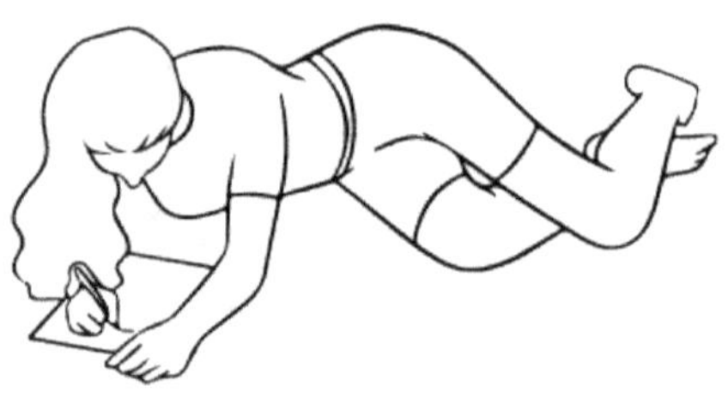

There she was,
Sitting alone under the tree,
Losing hope above the free,
That she was coping.

Leaving behind the abandonment by
her peers,
She is gearing up now,
With the balancing wheel of all the
ache,
She is taping everything.

Ignored by the social relationships,
She lost her battleship,
More somewhere,
With the criticism of her tone.

Breaking her comfort zone, turning to
her story,
Pleading for help, through her inner
self,
Flowing with the pressure, carrying a
bag full of goals,
Assuring her soul, there she was.

Addressed by her words, unknown of
the emotions to come.

2. The First Rain

It was Saturday morning,
With nature's warning,
Sky lightening, nature hustling,
Announced the first rain,
Filled the city with joy,
Birds chirping, leaves shaking,
From a child to an adult,
Everyone rejoiced,
All of it was full of content.

3. Framed in Shadows

It was a dark night,
Long and silent,
The provoked emotions are violent,
While the long haze passed to and forth.

The soul got stuck in a strange feeling,
Which stood like an iron railing,
It played a joker face,
Revealing into a lace.

Sometimes it was as simple as a shoe,
But felt complex like a fancy saree
border,
Still, the spark was ignited,

Where the fear of the unknown was
cited.

It rose to a plight of stairs,
All the time everything came unaware,
Repeatedly the agitation was seen,
Focused too much to not lean.

Termed as highly sensitive,
Always tried to be imperative,
Like the moonlight, to be constant,
The weirdness felt like an assistant.

4. The Notion of That Motion

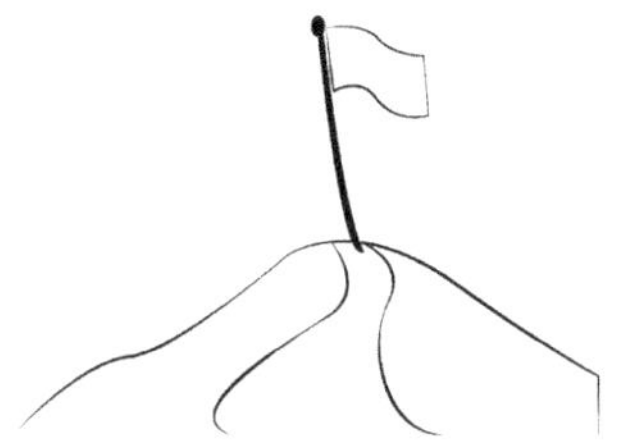

With sleepless nights,
There are thoughts without shine,
I had a ray of moonlight,
Trying to decipher those lines,
It was a motion to fit the notion of life,
She never knew it was time to dive,
Those shattered patterns were her
lanterns,
She was holding them tight,
The pillows hugged,
While the walls encouraged,
Until the moment left with thunder,
She received the signal,
Led her to a float of words,
And progressively she reached the
destination.

5. The Notion of That Motion II

In the dark,
Away from home,
There is a search,
For a peaceful dome.

Departed with the emotions,
She wanted to set a notion,
It began as a quiet girl,
To step on the journey.

Worried a bit,
Groomed like a lit,
Left the guilt,
Under her quilt.

She pursued every obstacle,
All resulting in a miracle,
It proved her a fierce woman,
Eventually became an inspiration for
the rest.

6. The Fictional Affairs

Amidst all the chaos,
The soul was tied up,
Hurrying within the time,
Buried under the shrine,
Everything from everyone was heard,
Fighting bravely till the end run,
It was only a matter of performance,
Missing out on feeling her importance,
Until the fictional characters explained,
'All affairs are tamed'.

7. The Uncertainty Kind

It isn't a new thing,
That life makes you overthink,
Not only once but numerous times,
You go out of the way,
To get things done right, yet still fail.

It isn't a new thing,
Where freedom is absent,
Within its presence
Where you feel choked,
Facing an endless end.

It isn't a new thing,
When you feel helpless,
Even when you have the most support,
Patience is needed the most,
To keep you from feeling lost.

In return, it is this lifetime,
Which eventually tells your worth.
Just take a deep breath,
Hold on and move on.

It isn't a new thing,
All things will be alright,
For life, with respect to your actions,
Will set everything right.

8. Losing the Translation

The clock struck midnight,
Everyone exchanged their wishes,
Partying to their fullest,
No one realised what was ahead of
them.

Next day,
Everyone continued to lay,
And things seemed normal,
People got back to work.

The city life made a feature,
Like a reality check,
Except for work and promotions,
Everything was mocked.

Some faced many lashes,
The spark exchanged to being dullest,
The destination was far yet it came,
Dried like a used bunch of hay.

The days felt cold and far too strict,
While progress smiled in the shadows,
Stuck between surviving and thriving,
Wishing, hoping, trusting deeply,
A dream under the heavy wood.

9. Balancing the Unsaid

As drops came and went,
The time flew by,
It was measured by the brain,
And considered by the heart.

Present events dissolved into the past,
Knocking the door was the future,
Each rise and dawn,
Made an addition to the story.

Lost were the days when we listened to
Lori (a cultural lullaby),
Faded was the shine of the late,
Yet nature showed a beautiful palette,
Amidst the chaos all around.

Mix bag of happiness, satisfaction,
Miseries and moments,
All around were the different phases of
time,
Don't get scared if you lose.

The path of the journey will be marked,
Exploring all the various arenas,
Be free and feel free,
Like the growth of a tree.

10. A Lock in the Pandemic

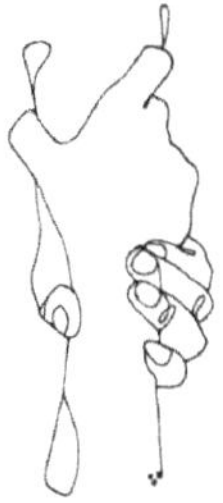

All of the dark felt hard,
Wondered if ever they could guard,
Screeching, Screaming,
Hoping, Dreaming.

The tendency was a shock,
To the admired goal,
They wanted to express to an entity,
But the soul was left ignored.

The extension was suffocating,
Causing the heart to relocate,
Fairy tales remained false,
Yet they hoped for an untitled
supportive entity.

Untitled fear and innocence evaporated,
Only stood was their dreams,
As much as they could wear the smile,
And reboot their journey.

They understood their imperfections,
Perhaps they will not strive for
perfection,
Instead, it was the contentment,
Faith and unity which healed all their
eyes saw.

11. A Quiet Reckoning

Within the world of hustle,
There is a tiny being,
She liked to be herself,
Yet always remained the excluded one.

Winds are blowing in all directions,
Tearing the inner dimensions apart,
Either questioned by soul or society,
She never got a chance to defend
herself.

Gradually the innocence faded,
And the day arrived when she chose to
be mute,
Seemed like a wooden box,

Filled with dark secrets along with
wishes.

No one knew the total was only two
wishes,
Wrapped with the realities via
expectations,
Never preferred a horse but performed
as a derby,
Drown under to pull up the most
satisfaction.

Later agreed with the presence of
incompleteness,
She moved to discover her self-worth,
Neither stepping back nor letting reality
decide.
Yet stayed in a dilemma between,
Knowing one's worth and being fair to
what relations?

12. The Repetitive Lessons

I wonder where you are,
Amidst the chaos,
Would you find me?
Amidst the monochrome,
Would you be my brown?

I wonder where you are,
Striving with the solitude,
Stretched longer than the longitude,
Would the scenario accept me?

I wonder where you are,
Looking towards the constellation,
Gazing at the process of distillation,
All over the galaxy.

I wonder where you are,
Who is not eternal,
And would not run away,
Regardless of the signal.

I wonder where you are,
Loving the fun ideas,
To be out of the head,
Living each moment passing by.

Still loving those black circles,
Under the eye,
In this unique peace of chaos,
Unable to think about you,
I wonder where you are.

13. The Demi-Actions

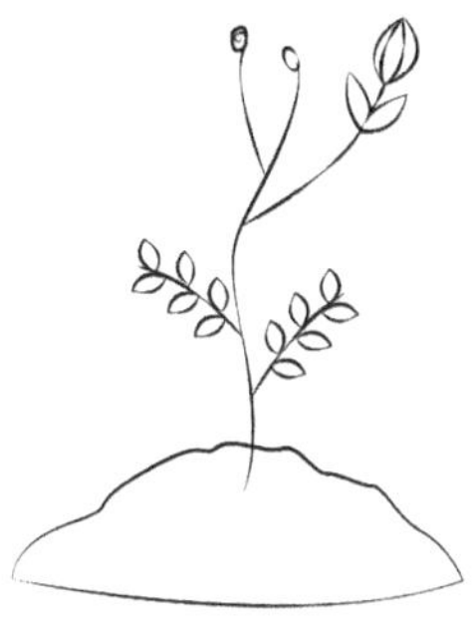

I hear the howling,
Fighting the heavy air,
It tries to stay alive,
In warmth that doesn't care.

So few notice, so few mind,
The world around the changing times,
A new start must appear,
A hope, a change, to hold near.

Imbibing a temporary gene,
Who will be the younger one,
Licking ice candies,
Drinking cold drinks.

And here I sit, with those I love,
Under the sky, so wide above,
Waiting for the winds to play,
And bringing us peace at the end of the
day.

14. Living in the Dreamland

Gazing at the stars,
Wondering the unanswered,
I was off to dreamland,
Between those clouds.
The cool air felt like feathers,
Everything felt like magic,
Exempted was the tragic,
No pressure was seen.

That absence felt good,
I was the creator,
Of that virtual world,
Where everyone was united.
Where impractical became practical,
And, no one suffered.

Something popped like a pin in a
balloon,
And like other horses,
I was in the gallon,
Preparing for the insane competition,
In humankind,
Out of that dreamland,
Far from the dream.

15. The Magical Charm

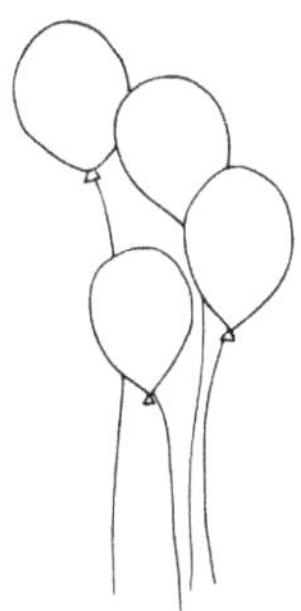

You are a glam,
To the kids,
Especially in the summer jam,
Similar to a fresh muffin without a lid.

You are so calm,
Disappearing the blur,
Quicker than the intercom,
No less than a fire extinguisher.

Regardless of the size of a palm,
Everyone enters your bio-bubble,
Gesturing a *salaam*,
And forgetting the daily rubble.

Maybe,
You are known as the ''world of magic''
Covering the tragic,
You are a clove of garlic,
Boosting the major's immunity.

16. The Echoes of You

You are heavy yet empty,
Don't be so,
Let things pass by,
And they will go.

You are such an immense realisation,
We doubt our organisation,
A million things happen,
Yet years roll over to understand the
blacken.

Waiting for it to pass by,
Such darkness is sly,
You are still the same and distant,
Rolling over like an assistant,
Considering you as a reflection,
We wonder if you are a deflection.

17. The Shooting Star

Soaking the energy from the cosmos,
Greyscaling a new pattern,
Tangling around the neck,
Soothing my head.

Took all my lethargy,
With eyes open wide,
Nothing could hide,
Muffled against the cotton,
Intertwining the button.

The colours of shades blurred,
In the way,
It was never understood again,
Along the warmth of the shooting star.

18. The Ecstasy

Yeah, I know it is too repetitive,
Yeah, I know I wonder all the time,
About you or something more colourful,
You both can be competitive.

Yeah, I know it stretches beyond
possible,
Yeah, I know it is no less than a tornado,
Neither the shine nor the play-doh,
I will always love you, double.

O my multi-talented euphoria,
Can I name you my forever Gloria?
I promise to never leave you,
The brightness even for the darkness,
My only dopamine.

19. Over-Forever

Always available for you,
I steal time at every blue,
Wondering, pondering,
Slimming, dimming,
Would you care?

Always available for you,
I think I oversee so much,
Is that enough or extra?
Or the physical being,
Simply being relentless?

Always available for you,
I can be an overthinker,
Overachiever, a little extra,

Yet, after so many *overs*,
Was the innocent boundary over,
Forever?

20. The Shiny Bling

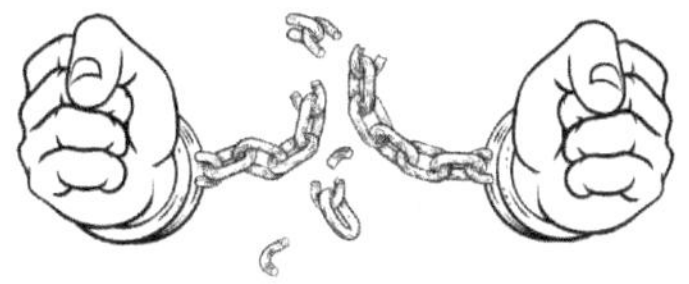

A swap of wind here,
A whirl of air there,
You are a burning sensation,
With different feelings,
I let you go,
Now and always,
Regardless of my wish,
I let you go,
When you are busy,
And,
You hurt my eyes,
With all your shiny bling.

21. Breaking the Limitations

Like the lost baby,
Like the scared baby,
I imagine a cradle,
Thousands of miles apart,
Self-consolation shaped like a ladle,
Even the closest feel,
Million galaxies away,
While all this time,
A ball of mud,
Dark and coarse,
Rolled here and there,
In a shape with no definition.

Like the cursor hovering there,
Waiting for you to be aware,
Future opportunities might knock you,
Do not fear to take a step back!

Gratitude to my Readers

Dear Reader,

Thank you for making me an author! As you close the final page of Whispers Across Tongues, I want to thank you for embarking on this journey with me. These poems are pieces of my heart—fragments of a soul that has wandered through self-doubt, love, heartbreak, and hope. It is through your eyes and emotions that these words come alive.

Every poem holds a story, but it is your interpretations, your reflections, that give them meaning beyond what I could have imagined. For that, I am deeply grateful. To those who have ever felt lost, this book is my hand reaching out to you. To those who have found their way, your journey is an inspiration to many.

Thank you for allowing my words to be a part of your life, even if just for a moment. Your time, your connection, and your support mean everything to me as a writer.

May you carry the whispers of these pages with you and continue to grow into the vision you hold for yourself.

With heartfelt gratitude,
Jill